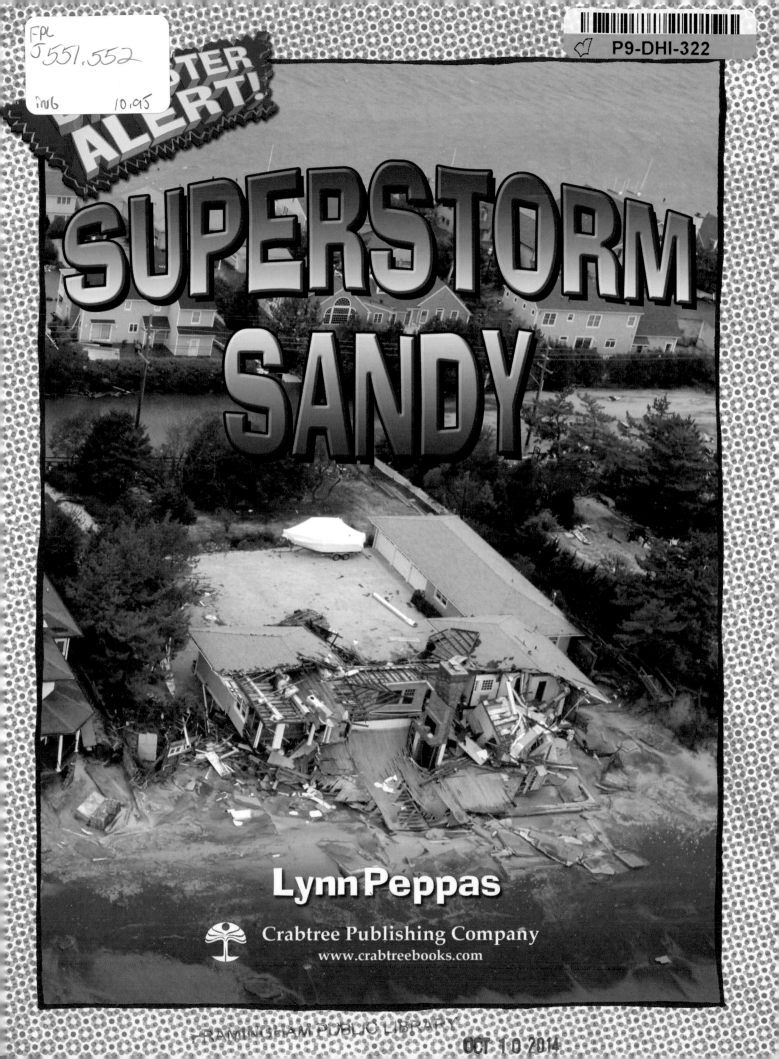

P9-DHI-322

DISASTER ALERT!

SUPERSTORM SANDY

LynnPeppas

Crabtree Publishing Company
www.crabtreebooks.com

presented by:

Crabtree Publishing Company

www.crabtreebooks.com

Author: Lynn Peppas

Project coordinator: Kathy Middleton

Editors: Kathy Middleton, Wendy Scavuzzo, Kelly Spence

Indexer: Wendy Scavuzzo

Design: Tammy McGarr

Photo research: Crystal Sikkens

Production coordinator and prepress technician: Tammy McGarr

Print coordinator: Margaret Amy Salter

Cover: The Ferris wheel and the Dominator spire are all that is left standing at the Fun Town Amusement Park in Seaside, N.J., after Superstorm Sandy hit.

Title page: An aerial view of the New Jersey coast shows a home badly damaged by Superstorm Sandy.

Contents: Thousands of people had to evacuate their homes in order to stay safe during Superstorm Sandy. The American Red Cross was one of many agencies that set up temporary shelters to help evacuees, such as Candice Haugland of Seaside Heights, N.J., and her nieces, eight-year-old Amy Hoopingarner and two-month-old Nora Remington.

Photographs:

American Red Cross: Les Stone: front cover,pages 3, 14, 42 (bottom);
    Talia Frenkel: pages 15, 41
Associated Press: pages 8, 18, 27 (bottom), 34, 42 (top)
FEMA: Sean Kerr: page 10; Patsy Lynch: page 23; Andre R Aragon:
    page 31; Andrea Booher: page 33 (background); Ryan Courtade:
    page 33 (inset); Jocelyn Augustino: page 35; Liz Roll: page 43
Getty Images: Michael Heiman: pages 36, 37
The Image Works: ©The Star-Ledger / Ed Murray: page 20; ©The
    Star-Ledger / Aristide Economopoulos: page 21
Keystone Press: ZUMAPRESS.com: pages 9 (top), 16, 25, 27 (top),
    28, 47; CARV/AKM-GSI: page 45
nationalaltas.gov: page 30 (bottom left)
Shutterstock: Jannis Tobias Werner: page 5; meunierd: pages 6,
    13 (bottom); Kobby Dagan: page 11; Globe Turner: pages 24, 39 (top),
    40; Rainer Lesniewski: page 26; GrabMaps: pages 30 (top left), 32;
    Daryl Lang: page 30 (right); Leonard Zhukovsky: pages 38–39;
    FloridaStock: page 44
U.S. Air Force photo/Master Sgt. Mark C. Olsen: pages 19, 22
Wikimedia Commons: New Jersey National Guard: page 1; NASA:
    page 4; US Navy: page 9 (bottom); David Shankbone: page 12;
    Vicpeters: page 13 (top); The National Guard: page 17; Thomas Good:
    page 29

Library and Archives Canada Cataloguing in Publication

Peppas, Lynn, author
    Superstorm Sandy / Lynn Peppas.

(Disaster Alert!)
Includes index.
Issued in print and electronic formats.
ISBN 978-0-7787-1193-3 (bound).--ISBN 978-0-7787-1195-7 (pbk.).--
ISBN 978-1-4271-8942-4 (pdf).--ISBN 978-1-4271-8940-0 (html)

    1. Hurricane Sandy, 2012--Juvenile literature. 2. Disaster
victims--United States--Juvenile literature. 3. Rescue work--United
States--Juvenile literature. I. Title. II. Series: Disaster alert!

HV636 2012.U6P47 2014   j363.34'922   C2013-907581-X
                                                     C2013-907582-8

Library of Congress Cataloging-in-Publication Data

Peppas, Lynn.
 Superstorm Sandy / Lynn Peppas.
   pages cm. -- (Disaster alert!)
 Audience: 008-011.
 Audience: Grade 4-6.
 ISBN 978-0-7787-1193-3 (reinforced library binding) -- ISBN 978-0-7787-
1195-7 (pbk.) -- ISBN 978-1-4271-8942-4 (electronic pdf) -- ISBN 978-1-4271-
8940-0 (electronic html)
 1. Hurricane Sandy, 2012--Juvenile literature. I. Title. II. Series: Disaster
alert!

 QC944.2.P47 2014
 551.55'20974090512--dc23

                                                     2013043396

Crabtree Publishing Company

www.crabtreebooks.com   1-800-387-7650

Printed in Canada/012014/BF20131120

Published in Canada
Crabtree Publishing
616 Welland Ave.
St. Catharines, ON
L2M 5V6

Published in the United States
Crabtree Publishing
PMB 59051
350 Fifth Avenue, 59th Floor
New York, New York 10118

Published in the United Kingdom
Crabtree Publishing
Maritime House
Basin Road North, Hove
BN41 1WR

Published in Australia
Crabtree Publishing
3 Charles Street
Coburg North
VIC, 3058

Table of Contents

What is a Hurricane?

Superstorm Sandy was one of the largest and most destructive Atlantic hurricanes ever recorded in history. In late October of 2012, the massive hurricane caused devastation to thousands of miles stretching from Jamaica to the northeastern part of the United States. Massive flooding in U.S. states along the eastern seaboard led to the outbreak of electrical fires and huge power outages. More than 200 people were killed and thousands more were evacuated during the disastrous seven-day storm.

What is a Natural Disaster?

A **natural disaster** is a destructive event created by nature. It can destroy people's communities, homes, and even take lives. Natural disasters, including hurricanes, are closely watched by weather scientists called **meteorologists**. While meteorologists can warn people about a possible natural disaster, there is nothing they, or anyone, can do to stop it from coming.

What is a Hurricane?

A **hurricane** is a spinning or rotating storm with powerful winds and heavy rainfall. Hurricanes form and grow over tropical oceans where wind and lots of warm water fuel the storm. When hurricanes make **landfall**, or move onto land, they start to die out or disappear. But, long before they reach land, their fierce winds and heavy rain can have devastating effects. Breakneck winds can reach from speeds of 74 mph (119 km/h) up to 155 mph (249 km/h) or greater. Over the warm ocean, a hurricane can grow from a **diameter** of 62 miles (100 km) to a massive 2,000 miles (3,219 km). At its greatest size, Sandy grew to be almost 1,000 miles (1,609 km) in diameter.

Hurricane Sandy swirls off the southeastern United States in this satellite image from October 28, 2012.

Hurricane Sandy caused more than eight million homes to lose power in 17 states on the eastern seaboard.

Superstorm Status!

As the threat of Hurricane Sandy loomed over the eastern seaboard of the United States, many journalists and TV broadcasters began calling Sandy a "superstorm." While superstorm is not an actual scientific term, **media** outlets often use the term to describe an extremely strong and destructive storm.

Frankenstorm

Hurricane Sandy was also nicknamed "Frankenstorm." The nickname stuck as the storm made landfall in the United States on October 29—a date very close to Halloween. Also, Sandy was made up of two different storms that came together to create a monster hurricane, much like the creation of the monster in the famous book *Frankenstein*. And, like a monster, the storm was terrifying, unpredictable, deadly, and destructive.

How Sandy Formed

Superstorm Sandy started out in warm tropical waters off the west coast of Africa in the Atlantic Ocean in the fall 2012 hurricane season. But, unlike most hurricanes, Sandy did not turn to the northeast into cooler waters and die out. Instead the storm met with unusual weather conditions that strengthened its power, bringing terrible destruction to the Caribbean Islands and the east coast of the United States.

Tropical Depression

The area surrounding the Caribbean Sea and Caribbean Islands of Cuba, Jamaica, and Haiti was experiencing a low pressure weather system. Together the rain and thunderstorms created the perfect conditions for a hurricane. The air pressure continued to drop and the system grew larger. By October 22, it had become a **tropical depression**, which is a storm with winds that blow for a full minute at speeds up to 38 mph (61 km/h).

Tropical Storm Sandy

As the air pressure remained low around the Caribbean, the tropical depression grew even larger with more thunderstorms. Six hours after being classified as a tropical depression, Sandy was upgraded to a **tropical storm** with destructive wind speeds of 39–73 mph (63–118 km/h). Once a storm has been classified as a tropical storm, it is given a name, and this one was called Sandy. Superstorm Sandy had begun.

Tropical storm winds have the power to break tree branches, knock down trees, and cause damage to buildings.

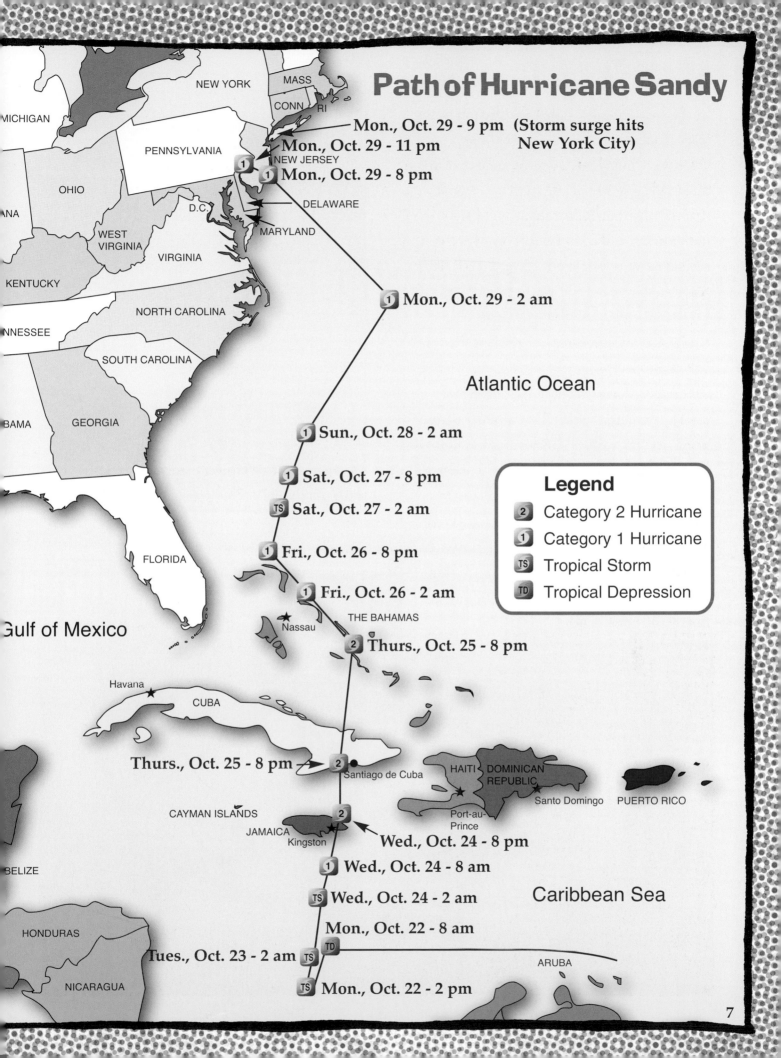

Path of Hurricane Sandy

Mon., Oct. 29 - 9 pm (Storm surge hits New York City)

Mon., Oct. 29 - 11 pm

Mon., Oct. 29 - 8 pm

Mon., Oct. 29 - 2 am

Atlantic Ocean

Sun., Oct. 28 - 2 am

Sat., Oct. 27 - 8 pm

Sat., Oct. 27 - 2 am

Legend
2	Category 2 Hurricane
1	Category 1 Hurricane
TS	Tropical Storm
TD	Tropical Depression

Fri., Oct. 26 - 8 pm

Fri., Oct. 26 - 2 am

THE BAHAMAS

Nassau

Thurs., Oct. 25 - 8 pm

Gulf of Mexico

Havana

CUBA

Thurs., Oct. 25 - 8 pm

Santiago de Cuba

HAITI   DOMINICAN REPUBLIC

Port-au-Prince

Santo Domingo   PUERTO RICO

CAYMAN ISLANDS

JAMAICA   Kingston

Wed., Oct. 24 - 8 pm

Wed., Oct. 24 - 8 am

Wed., Oct. 24 - 2 am

Caribbean Sea

Mon., Oct. 22 - 8 am

Tues., Oct. 23 - 2 am

ARUBA

HONDURAS

NICARAGUA

Mon., Oct. 22 - 2 pm

BELIZE

Sandy Upgraded to Hurricane

In the early morning hours of October 24, tropical storm Sandy officially became a Category 1 hurricane when its winds began to travel up to 74 mph (119 km/h). It was also on that day that Sandy first made landfall on the southeastern coast of Jamaica, near Kingston, with wind speeds of about 85 mph (137 km/h).

Hurricane Categories

Hurricanes are measured on a scale called the Saffir-Simpson hurricane wind scale. Hurricanes are classified into one of five categories— Category 1 being the weakest and Category 5 being the strongest. Once a storm has been classified as a hurricane, its threat of damage is measured by its wind speeds.

Saffir-Simpson Hurricane Scale		
Category	Wind Speed *	
	mph	km/h
5	157 +	252 +
4	130-156	209-251
3	111-129	178-208
2	96-110	154-177
1	74-95	119-153
Non-Hurricane Classifications		
Tropical Storm	39-73	63-118
Tropical Depression	less than 38	less than 62

*Wind speeds must remain constant for a period of one minute.

Hurricane-speed winds sent huge waves crashing into coastal towns in the Caribbean Islands, such as Kingston, Jamaica, shown here.

Sandy in the Caribbean

On October 25, Hurricane Sandy again made landfall near Santiago, Cuba. At that time, the storm's wind speeds were at the higher end of a strong Category 2 hurricane. More destruction followed as the storm moved across the Bahamas and weakened to a Category 1 hurricane. Landfall over the Bahamas caused Sandy to lose strength, and she was briefly downgraded from a hurricane to a tropical storm. But, by October 27, as the storm spun over warm, tropical waters off the northern coast of Florida, Sandy once again exploded into a Category 1 hurricane.

Superstorm Sandy severely damaged homes and buildings during its landfall in Cuba on October 25, 2012.

Two Storms Combine

Almost all hurricanes turn in a northeast direction and die out over cooler ocean waters– but not Sandy. An area of high pressure over the Gulf of Mexico, and another high-pressure system to the northeast of Hurricane Sandy, steered her on an offshore path along the eastern seaboard of the United States. Sandy collided with a **Nor'easter** storm system coming from the west, and the two storms combined to make a much larger storm. When a hurricane combines with another storm system, it is called the **Fujiwhara effect**.

Preparing for Sandy

After Sandy made landfall in Jamaica, the storm gained even more strength. Its path of destruction continued the next day as it made landfall on the southeast corner of Cuba. By the time Sandy left the Caribbean, the powerful hurricane had claimed the lives of more than 70 people.

U.S. Prepares for the Worst

As news spread about Sandy's path of destruction through the Caribbean, Americans were warned that the hurricane was heading toward the U.S. eastern seaboard. President Barack Obama worked with the Federal Emergency Management Agency (FEMA) and other government departments to prepare for when the hurricane would make landfall on U.S. soil.

The Department of Energy organized emergency responders to be ready to restore electricity if a major power outage occurred. The Department of Agriculture advised Americans about food safety and to make sure they had food and water on hand that did not need to be refrigerated. On October 27, more than 61,000 members of the U.S. National Guard were brought in to coastal communities to help in the event of a disaster.

FEMA workers help American citizens before, during, and after natural disasters such as Superstorm Sandy.

New York Prepares...

New York mayor Michael Bloomberg ordered a mandatory, or required, evacuation of approximately 375,000 people from the coastal areas of New York City, including lower Manhattan, Coney Island, and Queens. He recommended that people stay with family members outside of the evacuation area, or remain in one of more than 70 shelters set up by the city. In the evening on October 27, the Metropolitan Transportation Authority (MTA) shut down New York City's public transit system. The city's 1,750 public schools and many businesses were closed on October 28.

Shelves in many grocery stores, such as these in Manhattan, were picked clean as people prepared for Sandy to arrive.

(above) On October 27, all subway systems in New York were closed before Hurricane Sandy struck.

Flooding

A hurricane is one of nature's most destructive disasters. It can cause extensive damage to coastal communities even before it makes landfall. Hurricanes cause a surprising number of dangers to communities, such as storm surges and flash floods.

Flash Flood

A flash flood happens very quickly, from within a few minutes to up to six hours after a heavy rainfall begins. During a hurricane, flash floods occur when an enormous amount of rain falls or a storm surge pushes a large amount of water ashore. In city areas, storm drains and sewers usually take **excess**, or extra, water away. Too much water overflows drains and sewers and flooding covers roads and transportation routes.

Flooded streets make it very difficult for people to escape, or emergency crews and vehicles to move around. Sandy was made up of many thunderstorm systems, and the storm dumped a lot of water when it made landfall. The heavy rainfall and the storm surge created flash floods in areas such as Lower Manhattan in NYC.

A flash flood from Manhattan's East River covered nearby Franklin D. Roosevelt Drive.

Sandy's Storm Surge

Before making landfall, Superstorm Sandy caused coastal flooding from destructive storm surges all along the east coast from Florida to Maine. A storm surge is an unusual rise in **sea level** waters caused when the low-pressure center of a hurricane, called the **eye**, sucks water up, forming a huge bulge or mound of raised water. As the hurricane moves toward land, it pushes the mound of water along in front of it and on to the shore as it approaches land. Hurricane Sandy created a large and powerful storm surge that rose to a height of about 13 feet (4 m). Sandy's surge was almost twice as high as any other storm surge that had hit the New York/New Jersey coast in the past 100 years.

(above) Underground areas such as parking garages and subway systems were the first to be flooded in New York City.

Sandy did not make landfall on southeastern coastal states, but some areas there, including Miami, Florida, still experienced flooding from the storm surge.

Supersizing Sandy

Hurricane Sandy made landfall in New Jersey and New York at the worst possible time. High tides caused by the full moon created an even higher storm surge. The storm surge and high winds caused large power outages. In some areas, power was not restored until weeks later.

High Tides Work with Sandy

A **tide** is the regular rise and fall of sea levels caused by the pull of gravity from the Moon and the Sun, and the rotation of Earth. At certain times of the day, the Sun and Moon's force of gravity pull ocean waters upward, bringing higher tides of water to shores such as at New Jersey and New York. A normal high tide causes about a 4-foot (1.2 m) difference in the height of the water. Unfortunately, Sandy—with its already high storm surge—made landfall during high tide.

Full Moon Effect

During a full moon, the Moon is **situated**, or positioned, at its closest to Earth. This makes its gravitational pull even stronger, and the tide even higher. On October 29, 2012, the full moon brought the already high tide of water up about another foot (30 cm). Altogether, the storm surge, high tide, and full moon brought terrible flooding to the coastal areas of New Jersey and New York.

Rescue teams in Mount Laurel, NJ, used front-end loaders and dump trucks to reach residents who were stranded by Sandy's storm surge.

Powerless!

A hurricane's strong winds have enough power to knock down large trees, which can break power lines and cause a power outage. During the height of Superstorm Sandy, more than eight million Americans lost power in their homes. Five days later, more than three million people still did not have power. Further electrical damage was caused by saltwater floods. Salt **corrodes**, or breaks down and eats away, objects it comes in contact with. In New York and New Jersey, the saltwater driven ashore by Sandy ate away at the outer insulation that surrounded electrical wires which also caused power outages.

After Hurricane Sandy, some New York City residents, such as those living on Staten Island, had to live without power for more than a week during the cold month of November.

Saltwater floods make the cleanup of electrical systems even more difficult. When saltwater drains or dries up, it leaves dry salt behind. Salt conducts electricity, which means it allows electricity to flow through it. This makes electrical transformers and other machinery flooded by saltwater dangerous to handle. They have to be cleaned with fresh water first to get rid of the salt, then dried before they can be used again safely.

Sand and Snow

Days before Superstorm Sandy made landfall on the coast of New Jersey and New York, its journey along the southeastern shorelines caused destruction in other states including Florida, Georgia, and North Carolina.

Florida Feels Sandy

Even though Superstorm Sandy was about 200 miles (322 km) away from the coast of Florida, its tropical storm winds and thunderstorms were felt from October 25–27. The storm surge created flooding in some coastal areas and Fort Lauderdale's ocean-view roadway A1A was flooded for a stretch of about 2 miles (3 km). Almost 9,000 residents lost power due to strong winds toppling trees and downing power lines. Other coastal communities, such as Hollywood Beach, were partially flooded during high tide due to the storm surge.

Massive waves from Sandy's storm surge covered Florida's popular east coast highway A1A with water and sand, making it impossible for people to travel on.

Snow in Mid-Atlantic States

Superstorm Sandy did not affect all east coast states in the same way. Due to the Fujiwhara effect (see page 9), Sandy and a Nor'easter from the west joined together to create a powerful winter storm. The storm affected the Appalachian Mountain range and hit Virginia, West Virginia, Maryland, and parts of Tennessee. The blizzard began on October 29 and dumped more than 3 feet (1 m) of heavy snow in some areas. The weight of the snow caused thousands of trees to fall across and snap power lines, creating power outages in more than 120,000 homes in West Virginia alone. Major highways, schools, and businesses were shut down while rescue crews struggled to help those stranded without power.

The resulting extremely heavy snowfall in some Mid-Atlantic states, such as West Virginia (shown here), caused trees and power lines to break and roofs to cave in.

First American Lives Lost

The first Americans to lose their lives to Sandy were not even on land when the tragic accident happened. They were sailing on the Atlantic Ocean on the HMS *Bounty*. This 180-foot (55 m) long American sailing ship was modeled after a merchant vessel built from the 1700s. The captain of the ship and 16 crew members were sailing from New London, Connecticut, to St. Petersburg, Florida. The HMS *Bounty* was sailing 90 miles (145 km) off the coast of North Carolina when 70 mph (113 km/h) winds and 25-foot (8 m) high waves sank the ship in the Atlantic Ocean on October 29, 2012. One woman and the captain of the ship drowned. They were the first American fatalities of Superstorm Sandy.

Landfall: New Jersey

Superstorm Sandy made landfall for the first time on U.S. shores around 8 p.m. on October 29, 2012, at the coastal city of Brigantine, New Jersey—near Atlantic City. But the destructive storm surge from Superstorm Sandy arrived on New Jersey shores six hours before the actual hurricane made landfall.

Mandatory Evacuation

New Jersey governor Chris Christie declared a state of emergency for New Jersey on October 27. Residents and businesses on the **barrier islands**, from Sandy Hook South to Cape May, were under a mandatory evacuation order. People had to leave the area by 4 p.m. on October 28. People could choose to stay with friends or relatives farther inland, or at county shelters. Governor Christie also warned all New Jersey residents to prepare for power outages to last up to ten days.

"*...I am urging all New Jerseyans to take every possible and reasonable precaution to ready themselves for the storm's potential impact. That means having an emergency action plan for their families and other loved ones... and avoiding unnecessary risks in the severe weather, including staying off of the roads.*"
—Governor Chris Christie, 11 a.m., Oct. 27

New Jersey governor Chris Christie is shown here urging New Jersey citizens to take every precaution for the incoming superstorm.

Seaside Heights

Seaside Heights is a **borough** in Ocean County, New Jersey, on the Barnegat Peninsula. In the summer, it is a popular tourist attraction with sandy beaches, **boardwalks**, and amusement parks. The once-popular tourist destination was pounded by Superstorm Sandy's storm surge, high winds, and waves on October 29. Almost every home and business in Seaside Heights was damaged or destroyed by the storm. The 300-foot-long Casino and Funtown piers, which offered amusement park rides, food stands, and games, were destroyed, along with most of their rides. The JetStar roller coaster was torn from Casino Pier and stood upright in the shallow ocean water.

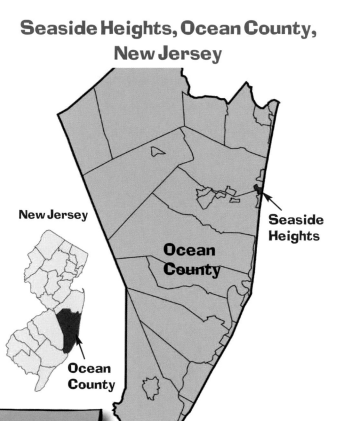

Seaside Heights, Ocean County, New Jersey

New Jersey

Ocean County

Ocean County

Seaside Heights

The Funtown Pier was rebuilt and opened again Memorial Day weekend on May 24, 2013. Unfortunately, not even a year after Sandy destroyed the famous boardwalk, it was brought to the ground again by a raging fire on September 12, 2013.

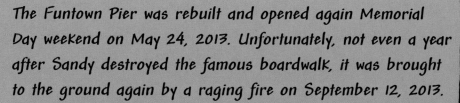

The JetStar roller coaster in the ocean was one of the most famous images newspapers and television broadcasts used to show the terrible destruction.

Sea Bright Devastation

Even though Governor Christie declared a state of emergency and ordered a mandatory evacuation, some residents chose not to leave their homes. Many remembered warnings about other tropical storms that turned out to be less severe than expected and thought it would be the same with Sandy. Unfortunately, in some areas, it was even worse than expected.

Sea Bright

Sea Bright is a borough in Monmouth County, New Jersey. It is located on the Sandy Hook Peninsula, a barrier island in New Jersey. Sandy destroyed almost every home and every business in the small community of 1,400. Even though the community had been ordered to evacuate by 4 p.m on October 28, some residents decided to stay in their homes during the hurricane. Some believed the storm was not going to be as disastrous as weather **forecasters** predicted.

Sea Bright, Monmouth County, New Jersey

Sea Bright

New Jersey

Monmouth County

Monmouth County

Residents who decided to stay in Sea Bright, walk along the shore during Hurricane Sandy on Monday, October 29, 2012.

It Really Happened...

Twenty-six-year-old Sea Bright resident David Coniff knew he was supposed to evacuate his home on October 28. But he thought it would be fun to invite some of his friends to stay with him in his third-story apartment during the storm instead. David and his friends started to become scared when they saw a steamroller, a truck, and cars being swept away in the water by the powerful storm. One of David's friends said the cars floating by looked like they were toys. They got so scared that some of them wore life vests in the apartment during the storm. The next day, they found that all downtown businesses were destroyed and many houses had collapsed. They felt lucky to be alive.

"When the power went out and the fire department sirens went off and the waves were crashing into the building, I felt like we made a mistake to stay."
—Sea Bright resident David Coniff

Sea Bright mayor Dina Long surveys the damage done by Sandy as she walks along Ocean Avenue through sand piles and past a home knocked from its foundation.

Coastal Damage

As Superstorm Sandy battered the New Jersey coast, the storm surge measured more than 8 feet (2.4 m) above normal tide levels in some areas. It was the worst damage and destruction the New Jersey coast had ever experienced.

Mantoloking

Mantoloking, New Jersey, is a borough in Ocean County, located on the Barnegat Peninsula. Of the many communities affected by Hurricane Sandy, Mantoloking was one of the hardest hit. The Atlantic Ocean split the seaside community in two, and created a new water **inlet** where streets had once been. Sandy damaged almost every home in Mantoloking and left only about half standing. More than 50 houses were torn off their foundations and sent crashing into other homes.

Mantoloking flooded when the Atlantic Ocean surged through the area, carrying homes with it and creating a new water inlet.

It Really Happened...

Mantoloking residents Ed and Betsy Wright learned that Sandy had destroyed all ten of their neighbors' homes—but left their three-story home standing. While all the other homes had been carried away by the storm surge, the Wright's home suffered very little damage and even the windows remained unbroken. People call the Wright's home the "miracle house." It might have been part miracle that saved it from disaster, but it was also good planning on Ed Wright's part. Thirty years ago, Ed specially built his home to withstand hurricane weather. And it worked!

Union Beach

Union Beach is a borough in Monmouth County, on the coastal mainland of New Jersey. It was one of the many communities that suffered crippling destruction when Hurricane Sandy damaged 1,600 of the area's 2,100 homes. A two-story yellow beachfront home became a popular image used by *Newsweek* magazine and other media sources. The house had been cut in half by the storm, with one side of the house and the roof still standing and the other side completely torn away.

The famous image of the half-torn home made the cover of Newsweek *magazine for the November 26–December 3, 2012 edition.*

It Really Happened...

Union Beach suffered extensive damage from Hurricane Sandy. The cleanup took many months and the help of many volunteers from outside the community. On October 29, Union Beach borough's only K-8 public school, Memorial School, was flooded with more than 1 foot (30 cm) of water. There was so much damage that the school was closed for more than seven months, and students had to go to other schools in nearby towns. The water that flooded the school contained sewage, mud, and other contaminated debris. The flood water also caused the growth of mold, which causes health and breathing problems.

Inland Floods

New Jersey's coastal communities were the hardest hit, but Sandy also damaged many New Jersey communities farther inland. The huge storm surge from Hurricane Sandy pushed the waters in the Hudson River up and over the banks, creating flash floods in waterfront communities including Jersey City and Hoboken.

Hudson River Floods

The Hudson River flows through the states of New York and New Jersey. Fresh water drains from the Hudson River into the Atlantic Ocean at New York Bay. The lower Hudson is a **tidal estuary**, which means water levels rise and fall with the changing Atlantic Ocean tides. Hurricane Sandy's storm surge pushed large amounts of water into the bay and into the Hudson River. Fresh water that would normally drain out of the Hudson River was pushed back onto the river's shorelines, causing flooding in riverfront communities such as Hoboken and Jersey City.

"I just don't think anybody thought the flooding from Hurricane Sandy would be as bad as it was."
—Hoboken resident Melissa Pittard, Huffington Post interview

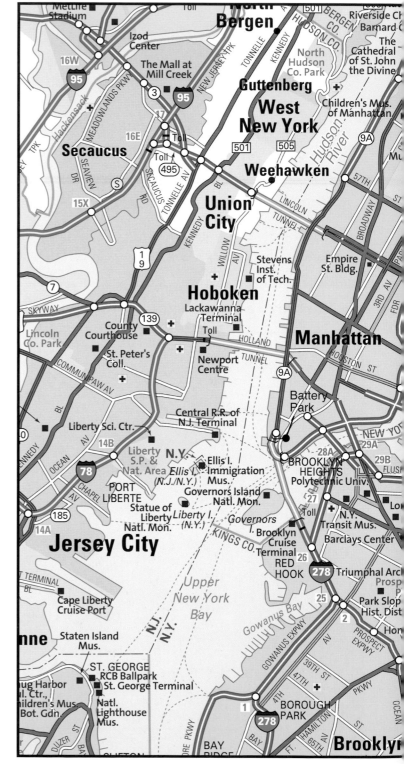

Hoboken

Hoboken is a city in New Jersey that lies on the west bank of the Hudson River. Residents living in ground floor apartments or homes in Zone A—a low-lying area in Hoboken—were asked to evacuate before Sandy hit. But the warning was not enough. On October 29, a flash flood hit the city, stranding about 20,000 residents in their homes.

"The flood came out of nowhere...it wasn't like, 'Oh, there's an inch of water, now there's two inches of water,' or "Oh my gosh, the water is getting higher.' There was no time for anything like that. All of a sudden we looked out and there was an ocean."
—Hoboken resident Theresa Wright, Business Insider interview

(above) The National Guard was called in to help people stranded in their homes by the flood waters, which contained contaminants such as sewage and oil.

The storm surge caused the Hudson River to flood the streets of Hoboken.

Landfall: New York City

New York City officials prepared for Superstorm Sandy by shutting down transportation systems, businesses, and schools. New York State governor Andrew Cuomo declared a state of emergency for all counties in the state of New York. New York City mayor Michael Bloomberg put the city's Coastal Storm Plan into action.

NYC Coastal Storm Plan

In 2000, New York City officials put together a Coastal Storm Plan to keep people as safe as possible in the event of a severe storm such as a hurricane or blizzard. The plan tracks the incoming storm, alerts people to the danger, and provides shelter for those who need to evacuate. It also helps clean up and rebuild damaged areas after the storm. Almost three million New Yorkers are expected to evacuate their homes and move to shelters when the Coastal Storm Plan is put in place.

NYC Flood Zones

Mayor Bloomberg ordered a mandatory evacuation for those living in Zones 1, 2, and 3. These zones are located along New York City's shorelines and in the low-lying areas of the city's five boroughs. After Superstorm Sandy occurred, city officials changed the boundaries of the zones.

New York City's five boroughs are Queens, Brooklyn, Manhattan, the Bronx, and Staten Island.

Shutting Down

Many areas of New York City were deserted long before Hurricane Sandy blew in. Subway, bus, and commuter train services were shut down on the evening of October 28—a full day before Hurricane Sandy hit. NYC ferries and airports were closed on October 29, making travel in or out of the city almost impossible. Bridges and tunnels within the mandatory evacuation areas were closed, and railway trains were moved to higher ground. Offices, stores, and schools were closed on October 29 in preparation for Sandy's arrival.

The storm caused 43 deaths in New York City and 60 altogether in the state of New York. It also destroyed or damaged about 305,000 homes. The damage in New York State was estimated to cost about $31 billion.

"[When evacuating] don't leave your pet at home, because you don't know when you can get back. So take your pet with you."
—Mayor Bloomberg prepares New Yorkers for the coming storm

The New York Stock Exchange was closed for two days during Sandy.

27

NYC's Transit System

Around 9 p.m. on October 29, the storm surge from Superstorm Sandy pushed into the East River. A continuous tide of saltwater overflowed the river banks, flooding New York City streets, tunnels, subways, and underground parking garages.

New York's Subway Flooded

More than five million people use the New York City transit system every day to go to work, school, and to move around the city. The storm surge flooded seven of NYC's subways with hundreds of millions of gallons of harmful saltwater. Many subway lines were not back up and running until more than a week after Sandy.

Saltwater from the Atlantic Ocean completely flooded subway stations such as South Ferry, shown here. This station was so badly damaged by the saltwater, it will have to be completely rebuilt.

Saltwater and Subways

Saltwater and subway lines are a dangerous combination. Salt eats away at metal parts, motors, and wires used to keep subway trains running safely. Salt can also ruin electronically operated signal systems used to stop trains from getting into accidents. After the flood waters were pumped out of the subway tunnels, workers still had to clean up the dried salt left behind. They also had to test flooded equipment to make sure it was running properly.

It Really Happened...

A Queens resident needed to return to work three days after Superstorm Sandy hit New York City. She walked 23 blocks to wait for a train, but found that many others were waiting for the same train and most were very angry. She decided to walk the other 47 blocks to work, which took her two hours. Then she had to walk the entire 70 blocks back home at the end of the day! Like her, thousands of others walked many miles to and from work every day until the NYC transit system was repaired.

" *The New York City subway system is 108 years old, but it has never faced a disaster as devastating as what we experienced [on the night of October 29].* "
—New York City transport director Joseph J. Lhota

New Yorkers on the Move

The lack of public transit did not stop many New Yorkers from getting around. Many walked or rode bicycles. Others drove vehicles. But too many vehicles on the roads caused traffic jams and congestion, so travel was often slow. It also caused a **gasoline** shortage. Many gas stations did not have power to operate their gas pumps. Gas stations that were operating had long lines of customers buying up all their gas. Some customers waited in line for up to five hours to buy gas during the week after the storm. Many people used social media to help them find open gas stations with shorter wait times.

Residents line up to buy gas at an open gas station on Bay Street in the Clifton section of Staten Island, NY.

Long Island

Long Island is another region of New York City that was hit especially hard by Superstorm Sandy. Thirteen residents on the island died as a result of the hurricane. It is the most populated island in the United States, and contains the NYC boroughs of Queens and Brooklyn, and two major airports. There are 9 bridges and 13 tunnels connecting Brooklyn and Queens to the mainland.

Hugh L. Carey Tunnel

The Hugh L. Carey Tunnel, formerly called the Brooklyn-Battery Tunnel, contains a roadway that travels under the East River, linking the boroughs of Brooklyn and Manhattan. On October 29, all tunnels linking boroughs and the mainland were shut down before Sandy struck.

The storm filled this tunnel with 86 million gallons (326 million liters) of flood water. The U.S. Army Corps of Engineers' National Unwatering SWAT team were sent in to pump out the water. They used the same high-powered water pumps that had been used in New Orleans after Hurricane Katrina in 2005.

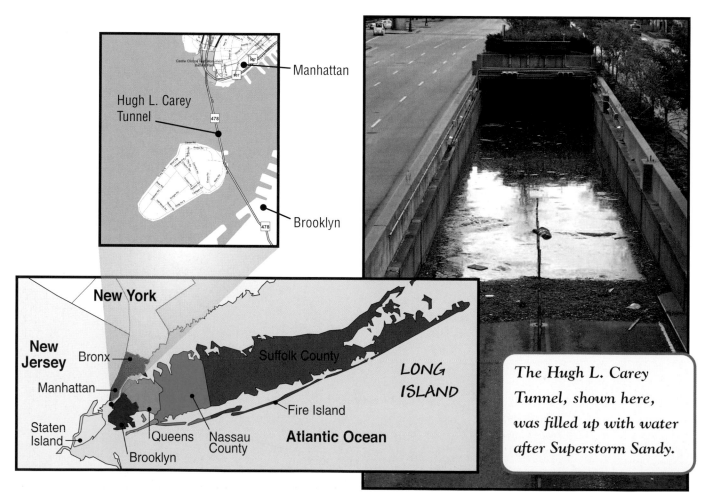

Manhattan

Hugh L. Carey Tunnel

Brooklyn

New York

New Jersey

Bronx

Manhattan

Staten Island

Queens

Brooklyn

Nassau County

Suffolk County

Fire Island

LONG ISLAND

Atlantic Ocean

The Hugh L. Carey Tunnel, shown here, was filled up with water after Superstorm Sandy.

Fire Island Washed Out

As Superstorm Sandy roared toward shore, about 120 Fire Island residents refused to evacuate. After the storm, they were stranded for days on this barrier island off the south shore of Long Island. Sandy had destroyed or heavily damaged eighty percent of Fire Island's homes and erased its beaches and sand dunes. **Washovers**—large amounts of sand and soil pushed by the water—had also been dumped onshore, destroying much of the beachfront property.

Fire Island home damaged by Hurricane Sandy

It Really Happened...

New York City's power outages lasted for many days after Superstorm Sandy and, in some places, for weeks. Many people used gasoline-powered generators for electrical power in their homes. One Oceanside, Long Island, resident ran a generator inside her garage for days after the storm. She didn't know that gasoline-powered motors, such as those in cars and generators, give off an odorless poisonous gas called carbon monoxide. The gas is not deadly outdoors because it mixes with the air. But, when enclosed in a garage attached to a home, the gas poisons all living things inside the home. Sadly, the woman and her three pets died when they were accidentally poisoned by carbon monoxide.

"...we always wanted a tree in the living room. Now we have our living room under the tree."
—Fire Island resident David Cloutier jokes about his destroyed summer home,
The New York Times

31

Breezy Point, Queens

New York City is surrounded by bodies of water such as the Atlantic Ocean, New York Harbor, the East River, and Jamaica Bay. The storm surge from Superstorm Sandy flooded many areas throughout the city. But, even when surrounded with so much water, many neighborhoods were threatened by fires.

A Tough Storm for Firefighters

The largest group of house fires started in Breezy Point, a community on the Rockaway Peninsula in the New York borough of Queens. Superstorm Sandy flooded the entire area around 7 p.m. on October 29 with about 4 feet (1.2 m) of rushing water. A house fire in the community began just before 8 p.m. Local volunteer and New York City firefighters could not drive their fire trucks through the flood waters. Strong winds spread the fire from house to house and many homes were burned to the ground before firefighters could put out the fires.

Map labels: Breezy Point Clubhouse, Highland Pl, Marshall Ave, Market, Bayside, 12th Ave, Palmer Dr, W. Market St, Ocean Ave, 12th Ave, Clinton Walk, Hillcrest Walk, Bedford Ave, Reid Ave, 10th Ave, 9th Ave, Oceanside Ave, 8th Ave, Rockaway Point Blvd, Utica Walk, Tioga Walk, Suffolk Walk, Queens Walk, Olive Walk, W End Ave, Irving Walk, 7th Ave, Essex Walk, Fulton Walk, Graham Pl, Gate, 4th Ave, Beach 222nd St, Breezy Point Blvd, Oceanside Av, Beach 227th St, Breezy Point Park

Fires caused by Superstorm Sandy destroyed hundreds of homes in states such as New Jersey and New York. Most of the fires in the two states started when saltwater touched electrical systems and sent off sparks that started fires. Electrical wires that were snapped by falling trees also started fires in buildings, as did candles used for light when the power went out. Chest-deep flood waters made it nearly impossible for firefighters to reach many of the houses to put out the flames.

It Really Happened...

Local volunteer firefighters were gathered in a community shelter at the Breezy Point Clubhouse on the evening of October 29. Some had left the firehouse next door because the building and the emergency vehicles had been flooded by the storm. The situation became worse when the clubhouse started filling up with smoke from the fires in the surrounding neighborhood. A few firefighters went back to the firehouse and managed to start up two fire trucks. They used the trucks to get the people in the clubhouse to safety. Around 11 p.m., other firefighters began to arrive at the blazing scene of the fires. At that time about 20 homes were ablaze. Three hundred firefighters worked together for about 12 hours to put out the fires. But, for many homes, it was already too late. They had burned to the ground.

Only ashes were left of more than 120 homes that were burned to the ground after Hurricane Sandy hit Breezy Point, NY.

Red Hook, Brooklyn

New York City is home to more than eight million people and has the largest population of any city in the United States. More than 375,000 New Yorkers had to leave their homes during Superstorm Sandy. Many came back to unbelievable loss and destruction.

Brooklyn

Brooklyn is a New York City borough with a population of more than two million people. Many people living near the waterfront areas were evacuated for the storm. Power was shut off to prevent electrical fires. Many homes and businesses were damaged when more than 5 feet (1.5 m) of flood waters rushed into the borough on October 29.

Flood-damaged Food

Red Hook is an old Brooklyn neighborhood that has become a popular shopping and eating spot. New Yorkers visit Red Hook to shop at the Fairway Market, located in a renovated waterfront coffee warehouse from the 1800s. During the flood and power outage, the market's food spoiled or was damaged, and displays and shelving were ruined. After four months of cleanup and renovation, the market reopened in March.

The Fairway in Red Hook, Brooklyn, is a popular grocery market. Below, dozens of carts loaded with spoiled and damaged foods and other products wait outside for garbage pickup.

Rebuilding Red Hook

Many Red Hook residents and business owners suffered hundreds of thousands of dollars in damage from Hurricane Sandy. But New Yorkers take pride in their abilities to join together and overcome these types of tough situations. Neighbors kept each other's spirits up and worked together to clean up after the storm. One group of volunteers, called the Red Hook Initiative, organized the community to assist older residents in removing ruined furniture from basements and ground floor homes. One Red Hook store owner generously gave out free bagels and coffee to volunteers and neighbors.

Victoria Tarpin, owner of Steve's Authentic Key Lime Pie, was determined to get back in business after Sandy flooded her Red Hook store.

It Really Happened...

The Gorham family—Ralph and Susan, and their 13-year-old son and 8-year-old daughter—made their living off selling lobster from their store called the Red Hook Lobster Pound. After Sandy came through, on October 29, more than 4 feet (1.2 m) of contaminated saltwater filled the store. The water stayed for about 12 hours, destroying walk-in refrigerators, $40,000 in lobster meat, cooking equipment, walls and floors, and the heating system. It also ruined the engine of their new food truck that was parked across the street. Their plans to expand the business had to be replaced with plans to rebuild it.

"I can replace my truck. I can't replace my kids. The rest is just money and time."
—Ralph Gorham, The New York Times

Manhattan Hospitals

The New York City borough of Manhattan is the smallest of the five boroughs, but it has the largest population of New Yorkers living there. It lies at the mouth of, and along, the Hudson River. It has an internationally famous business area and is home to the financial district of Wall Street, and such institutions as the New York and NASDAQ Stock Exchanges, the United Nations Headquarters, Times Square, New York City Hall, and New York University.

Hospital Evacuations

Not all people can simply pack up and leave when disaster threatens. Some people were being cared for in the hospital when Superstorm Sandy hit. Power outages made it unsafe for patients to remain there, so doctors, nurses, healthcare workers, and rescuers evacuated patients to other hospitals to continue caring for them. For those who were very ill, it was a risky move. But it was even more dangerous to stay.

New York area hospitals located in the evacuation zones used numerous ambulances to move ill patients to hospitals in safer areas of New York.

It Really Happened...

On October 29, 2012, about 300 patients were being cared for at New York University's Langone Medical Center. The hospital lost all power when Superstorm Sandy hit. Medical staff and rescuers had to carry the patients down dark stairwells because, without power, the elevators no longer worked. The first patients to be evacuated were 20 newborn babies, some of whom needed help breathing. About 20 ambulances waited outside the hospital to carry patients to other hospitals in safer parts of the city.

(above) Hospital workers carry a patient down the stairs of the NYU Langone Medical Center on the evening of October 29.

"...a couple of hours [after giving birth], things got a little hairy. The electricity started to flicker and the windows got shaky."
—Margaret Chu, a patient at Tisch Hospital who gave birth to a baby boy hours before Superstorm Sandy hit New York City, Associated Press

Staten Island

Staten Island experienced terrible flooding on October 29, 2012. Hurricane Sandy's storm surge pounded the area with the highest water levels in the entire state of New York.

New York Bight

A **bight** is a bend or indent in a coastal shoreline that forms a bay. The New York Bight forms an elbow-shaped indent from Cape May in New Jersey to the eastern tip of Long Island. The ocean floor of the bight is a continental shelf that is much shallower than the Atlantic Ocean. The shallow waters made the storm surge even higher and millions of tons of seawater were pounded onto the shore, flooding the coastal areas of Staten Island.

"Staten Island is at the end of, basically, a big funnel between New Jersey and New York."
—Andrew Ashton, a scientist at Woods Hole Oceanographic Institution, www.livescience.com

Sandy Hits Staten Island

Fifteen-foot waves on top of the record-breaking storm surge were devastating for Staten Island residents. More than half of the deaths Hurricane Sandy caused in New York City happened on Staten Island. Twenty-three people lost their lives, and 20 of those deaths were from drowning.

A photo taken on October 30 shows the flooded basement of a home in Staten Island. The day before, the water had reached 7 feet (2.1 m) deep, as shown by the waterline it left high on the wall.

Staten Island

Fresh Kills Park
NEW SPRINGVILLE
BRELLE AV
DONGAN HILLS
RICHMOND RD
SEAVIEW BL
HYLAN
Staten Island Mall
La Tourette Park
Moravian Cemetery
Lighthouse
Historic Richmond Town
Jacques Marchais Mus. of Tibetan Art
NEW DORP
NUGENT AV
MIDLAND BEACH
FATHER CAPODANNO
MILLER FIELD (Gateway)
NEW DORP BEACH
ARTHUR KILL
GIFFORD LA
OAKWOOD BEACH
GREAT KILLS
FOREST
RICHMOND RD
ELTINGVILLE
Great Kills Hbr.
GREAT KILLS PARK (Gateway N.R.A.)
HUGUENOT
HYLAN

7-foot (2.1 m) waterline

It Really Happened...

Oakwood Beach is a neighborhood on the east coast of Staten Island. The neighborhood holds the record for the highest recorded water level in New York during Hurricane Sandy. Water reached almost 10 feet (3.1 m) high in some homes. The New York State government offered to buy damaged properties from owners here and in other coastal areas. Building in these higher-risk areas will be restricted. One city worker named Joe Monte, who has lived in the area for 22 years, decided he would sell his home. He said they needed to feel safe and live a normal life again.

Staten Island Help

Hurricane Sandy's storm surge quickly carried more than 13 feet (4 m) of water to some areas of Staten Island. Many were stranded in their homes, surrounded by water. Twenty Staten Island residents drowned during Superstorm Sandy—more storm-related deaths than any other New York borough.

It Really Happened...

Seventeen-year-old Joseph Harasym became separated from his family on the evening of October 29 after a huge wave of water flooded their neighborhood. The power went out, and Joseph was trapped in his home in Midland Beach, Staten Island. Water filled the basement and quickly rose to the first floor, forcing a very scared Joseph to move up to the second floor. Rescuers still had not arrived by Tuesday morning, so he decided to swim to his friend's house about a block away. Joseph said the water was very cold, which made it hard for him to swim, so he stopped once to stand on a car roof to rest. He made it to the house where his friend, his friend's sister, another friend, and two family cats were stranded. They were all rescued later that morning by an adult family friend in a rowboat, and Joseph was reunited with his family.

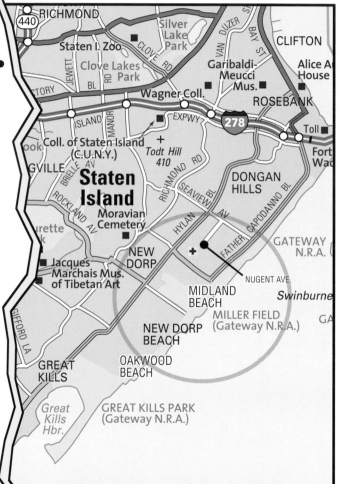

"I've been here 27 years and never, never, never has [this happened before]. We're almost a mile (1.6 km) away from the water—it's insane."
—Elizabeth Harasym, mother of Joseph Harasym, New York Daily News

Everyday Heroes

Emergency workers, including police officers, firefighters, and rescuers, did their best to save people—but there were so many that needed help. Sometimes ordinary citizens became heroes by putting their lives in danger to save others during Superstorm Sandy.

Red Cross volunteers brought "Sandy Kits" to families whose homes were destroyed during the hurricane. The kit included essentials such as a blanket, gloves, hand warmers, batteries, and a flashlight.

It Really Happened...

New Dorp Beach, Staten Island, resident Anthony Morotto became a hero during Superstorm Sandy. During the storm, he was on the second floor of his two-story home when he heard people screaming for help from the floodwaters outside. Thinking quickly, he tied a rope around his waist and pulled three of his neighbors to safety through the second-story window of his home.

41

Rebuilding After Sandy

In the aftermath of Sandy, Americans joined together to raise money and help rebuild people's homes and businesses. Government agencies such as FEMA, and charitable agencies such as the American Red Cross, have helped to rebuild what was lost in the storm.

Government Aid

The U.S. federal government established the Hurricane Sandy Rebuilding Task Force on December 7, 2012. The task force is paid by the government to repair homes and public works. The U.S. Senate approved more than $50 billion to help victims of Hurricane Sandy. The money will also go to the rebuilding of roads, bridges, and transit systems. Part of the funding will be used for the city-run NYC Build it Back program that helps homeowners, landlords, and tenants whose homes were damaged by Hurricane Sandy.

Charity Organizations

Many different charity organizations, such as the American Red Cross, raised money and organized volunteers to help after the disaster. The Red Cross sent about 5,000 workers to help Sandy victims. Altogether, charities raised approximately $400 million to help those affected by Hurricane Sandy. The American Society for the Prevention of Cruelty to Animals (ASPCA) raised over $1 million. Volunteers from this group rescued animals from flooded neighborhoods and provided care for hundreds of animals that had no owners or homes to go back to after the storm.

President Barack Obama visited New Jersey's governor Chris Christie to view the area and offer his support in the face of the disaster caused by Superstorm Sandy.

Some evacuation shelters, such as the one at Pine Belt Arena in Toms River, New Jersey, allowed pet owners to stay there with their animals.

Building It Better

FEMA studied the effects of Hurricane Sandy on coastal areas such as New Jersey and New York, and put together Advisory Base Flood Elevation (ABFE) maps. These documents help communities properly rebuild their homes to withstand any future natural disasters. State and local governments set **building codes**, which are rules for people who build or rebuild homes in low-lying coastal areas. The Base Flood Elevation (BFE) is the height that surface water reaches in a flood. Homes and buildings built above an area's BFE have a better chance of escaping damage from floods brought on by natural disasters such as hurricanes. New homes must also be built stronger to withstand hurricane force winds.

Superstorm Sandy destroyed buildings, homes, roads, and bridges. Workers began rebuilding as soon as possible, to help people get their lives back to normal.

Buyouts

New Jersey and New York state governments have offered to buy land and homes from people in areas that are thought to be too dangerous to live in. Buyouts are voluntary, which means homeowners do not have to sell their properties if they do not want to.

Rock musicians—some of whom had been born in areas devastated by Hurricane Sandy—put on a benefit concert to raise money for the relief effort. The 12-12-12 concert took place on December 12, 2012 (or 12-12-12) at Madison Square Garden in New York City. The concert featured performances by musicians such as Bon Jovi, Bruce Springsteen, Alicia Keys, and Kanye West. Money raised from the concert went to the Robin Hood Relief Fund for victims of Hurricane Sandy. The internationally televised concert raised over $50 million.

Future Superstorms

Some scientists believe that the damage and destruction from Hurricane Sandy is just the beginning of what to expect from superstorms in the future. As Earth's surface becomes warmer and sea levels rise, coastal communities around the world face the threat of even more devastating storms and floods.

Global Warming

Global warming is the rise in Earth's average surface temperature. Global warming is a natural process that happens over hundreds of thousands of years. It occurs from natural events such as volcanic eruptions. But many scientists worry that Earth is warming up too fast due to human-made pollution and the **greenhouse effect**. In the last 100 years, Earth's climate has warmed by about 1.4°F (0.8°C). Scientists predict that global warming in the next 100 years could increase at an even faster rate. Global warming causes the sea level to permanently rise as the water warms and expands. A rise in sea levels can spell disaster for coastal communities, especially during storms and storm surges. Scientists from around the world are studying the effects of global warming on Earth. They do not know exactly what will happen. Some believe that global warming will create fewer, but larger, and more destructive storms in the future. Others believe that larger hurricanes with heavier rains and stronger winds will happen more frequently.

Changing Jet Stream

Some scientists are looking at the possibility that global warming is weakening the **jet stream**. Jet streams are fast moving winds high above Earth's surface that form between two areas with large differences in temperature. As the Arctic becomes warmer, there is less difference in these temperatures, which makes the jet stream weaker. A jet stream moves weather systems such as storms. Weaker jet streams mean that storms such as Hurricane Sandy may last longer and do more damage.

Melting polar ice caps and rising sea levels increase the chance of coastal flooding around the world.

Preparing for the Future

U.S. president Barack Obama put together the President's Climate Action Plan in June 2013. The plan outlines steps to be taken to reduce greenhouse gas emissions in an effort to slow down global warming. The government also promised to increase renewable energy sources from the wind and Sun, and heat energy from within Earth. The plan also gives money to state and local governments to better prepare for future storms by strengthening roads, bridges, and coastal shorelines.

"...what we've learned from Hurricane Sandy and other disasters is that we've got to build smarter...(to) protect our homes and businesses, and withstand more powerful storms."
—President Obama's climate speech at Georgetown University in Washington, DC, on June 25, 2013

U.S. president Barack Obama promised to respond to the threat of climate change so that future generations of Americans will have a cleaner and safer environment.

Glossary

Note: Some boldfaced words are defined where they appear in the text.

barrier island A long, narrow strip of land that runs alongside a coast and often protects the main coast from destructive waves

boardwalk A long walkway that is built over sand or marsh

borough A village, town, or part of a large city that governs itself

contaminated Ruined by being made dirty or unfit for use

diameter A straight line that measures the distance across the center of a circle or round object

eastern seaboard The east coast of a landmass or country

evacuate Leave a dangerous area

forecaster A scientist who studies the weather to make predictions for future weather conditions

gasoline A type of liquid fuel used to power machines such as engines

greenhouse effect A process in which Earth's atmosphere traps the Sun's heat and prevents it from escaping back into space

inlet A small, natural bay or area of water that sticks out from a larger body of water and forms against a landmass

media The main way news and information is given to large numbers of people, such as through television, radio, and newspapers

meteorologist A scientist who studies the atmosphere and weather conditions on Earth

Nor'easter A strong northeasterly wind that brings powerful winter storms to the east coast of the United States and Canada

odorless Having no smell

sea level The average level of the surface of the sea in relation to land

sewage Unwanted waste that is carried away from homes in sewer systems

transformer A device that changes high voltage electricity that comes from a power plant to a lower voltage for use in the home

Learning More

BOOKS:

Challen, Paul. *Hurricane and Typhoon Alert!* Crabtree Publishing, 2004.

Gregory, Josh. *The Superstorm Hurricane Sandy*. Scholastic, 2013.

WEBSITES:

www.noaanews.noaa.gov
The National Oceanic and Atmospheric Administration is a U.S. government weather science agency. Their website offers photos, maps, videos, and updates on the effects of Superstorm Sandy.

www.enchantedlearning.com/subjects/weather/hurricane/
This Enchanted Learning website gives readers a full explanation of the science of hurricanes.

www.ready.gov/hurricanes
FEMA's website has a checklist of steps to take to prepare for a possible hurricane.

NYC mayor Michael Bloomberg signs in before holding a press conference in New York Public School 195k in Manhattan Beach, Brooklyn—a neighborhood hit hard by Hurricane Sandy.

Index